Indiana

Rich Smith

Visit us at
www.abdopublishing.com

Published by ABDO Publishing Company, 8000 West 78th Street, Suite 310, Edina, Minnesota 55439 USA. Copyright ©2010 by Abdo Consulting Group, Inc. International copyrights reserved in all countries. No part of this book may be reproduced in any form without written permission from the publisher. The Checkerboard Library™ is a trademark and logo of ABDO Publishing Company.

Printed in the United States.

Editor: John Hamilton
Graphic Design: Sue Hamilton
Cover Illustration: Neil Klinepier
Cover Photo: iStock Photo
Interior Photo Credits: AirPhoto-Jim Wark, Alamy, AP Images, Comstock, Corbis, Fort Hays State University's Sternberg Museum of Natural History (fish-within-a-fish), Getty, Granger Collection, Indiana Pacers, Indiana University, Indianapolis Colts, iStock Photo, Library of Congress, Lynne Whitehorn-Umphres, Mile High Maps, Mountain High Maps, North Wind Picture Archives, One Mile Up, and Peter Arnold Inc, Photo Researchers, RavenFire Media, Thomas Harper, and U.S. Postal Service.
Statistics: State population statistics taken from 2008 U.S. Census Bureau estimates. City and town population statistics taken from July 1, 2007, U.S. Census Bureau estimates. Land and water area statistics taken from 2000 Census, U.S. Census Bureau.

Manufactured with paper containing at least 10% post-consumer waste

Library of Congress Cataloging-in-Publication Data

Smith, Rich, 1954-
  Indiana / Rich Smith.
     p. cm. -- (The United States)
  Includes index.
  ISBN 978-1-60453-649-2
  1. Indiana--Juvenile literature. I. Title.

  F526.3.S656 2009
  977.2--dc22
                          2008051039

Table of Contents

The Hoosier State

Indiana's nickname is the Hoosier State. No one is sure what the name "Hoosier" means. But the people of this Midwestern state have liked calling themselves Hoosiers since the early 1800s.

Sports are very popular in Indiana. Each year the world's biggest auto race is held in the state. Indiana also is the home of great professional football and basketball teams. College basketball is especially popular in Indiana.

Much of Indiana is farm country. From its fertile fields come many favorite foods.

Steel is forged in Indiana. Some of it is used to make cars, appliances, and other products at factories across the state.

Much of Indiana is farm country. Corn and soybeans are the state's main crops.

Quick Facts

Name: Indiana is an English word meaning "Land of the Indians."

State Capital: Indianapolis

Date of Statehood: December 11, 1816 (19th state)

Population: 6,376,792 (16th-most populous state)

Area (Total Land and Water): 36,418 square miles (94,322 sq km), 38th-largest state

Largest City: Indianapolis, population 795,458

Nickname: The Hoosier State

Motto: The Crossroads of America

State Bird: Cardinal

Salem Limestone

Tulip Tree

Wabash River

State Flower: Peony

State Rock: Salem Limestone

State Tree: Tulip Tree

State Song: "On the Banks of the Wabash, Far Away"

Highest Point: Hoosier Hill, 1,257 feet (383 m)

Lowest Point: Wabash River, 320 feet (98 m)

Average July Temperature: 85°F (29°C)

Record High Temperature: 116°F (47°C), July 14, 1936, at Collegeville

Average January Temperature: 34°F (1°C)

Record Low Temperature: -36°F (-38°C), January 19, 1994, at New Whiteland

Average Annual Precipitation: 40 inches (102 cm)

Number of U.S. Senators: 2

Number of U.S. Representatives: 9

U.S. Postal Service Abbreviation: IN

Geography

Indiana is in the upper Midwest region of the United States. It is the 38th-largest state.

Long ago, a glacier once covered Indiana. When the earth's climate warmed, the glacier melted. It left behind some of the best soil in the nation.

Indiana has two major natural regions. The one in the northern part of the state is largely flat. The one in the south has rugged hills.

The Wabash River is Indiana's official state river. It is mostly a winding river enjoyed for its beauty.

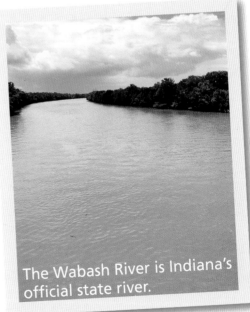

The Wabash River is Indiana's official state river.

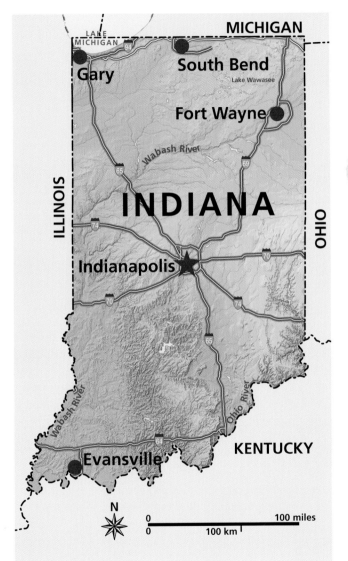

LAKE MICHIGAN

MICHIGAN

Gary

South Bend

Lake Wawasee

Fort Wayne

Wabash River

ILLINOIS

INDIANA

Indianapolis

OHIO

Wabash River

Ohio River

KENTUCKY

Evansville

N

0   100 miles
0   100 km

Indiana's total land and water area is 36,418 square miles (94,322 sq km). It is the 38th-largest state. The state capital is Indianapolis.

The Ohio River marks Indiana's border with Kentucky. In this picture, Indiana is on the left and Kentucky is on the right.

The Ohio River is a major waterway used mainly for commercial shipping. It serves as Indiana's border with Kentucky. But the Ohio River is not actually in Indiana. Just the shoreline belongs to Indiana. The water is Kentucky's.

Indiana's largest natural body of water is Lake Wawasee.

Other rivers in Indiana include the Kankakee, Maumee, Tippecanoe, White, Mississinewa, Eel, and Whitewater. The largest natural body of water entirely inside Indiana is Lake Wawasee. A tiny corner of one of the Great Lakes is within Indiana's northwest boundary. That is Lake Michigan.

Climate and Weather

Indiana has a continental climate. Summers are sticky hot while the winters are cold enough for snow. Only in the very southern part of the state are the winters more mild.

Yearly rainfall in Indiana averages 40 inches (102 cm). Thunderstorms often occur in Indiana. The state is sometimes struck by tornados and blizzards.

Each year Indiana has many thunderstorms.

July is Indiana's hottest month. The daytime temperature normally reaches a high of about 85°F (29°C). But the mercury once climbed to 116°F (47°C). It was Indiana's hottest day ever and it happened on July 14, 1936, at a place called Collegeville.

Indiana's coldest month is January. A daytime temperature of 34°F (1°C) is normal. The very coldest day on record was January 19, 1994, when the thermometer in the city of New Whiteland read -36°F (-38°C).

A winter blizzard in West Lafayette, Indiana, makes walking difficult for Purdue University students.

Plants and Animals

Indiana has very good soil. More than 120 kinds of trees grow in Indiana. Most common are hardwood varieties such as oak, hickory, maple, and elm. Pine and other softwood trees are rare.

The official tree of Indiana is the tulip tree. It has special qualities and historic importance to the state. Tulip trees grow fast and tall, and have sturdy wood. Native Americans used tulip trees to make canoes. Settlers used them to make homes.

Indiana's wildflowers are among the most beautiful in the world. These include pale purple coneflower, false sunflower, and black-eyed Susan. The state's official flower is the peony.

The tulip tree is Indiana's state tree. Its blossoms look like tulips.

Animals found in Indiana include chipmunks, opossums, minks, raccoons, muskrats, bats, badgers, rabbits, squirrels, mice, beavers, bobcats, coyotes, white-tailed deer, foxes, moles, river otters, and shrews.

Mouse

Many kinds of snakes live in Indiana. They include the black kingsnake, bull snake, garter snake, and rattlesnake. Other common reptiles are lizards and turtles. Among the state's amphibians are frogs, toads, salamanders, newts, and mudpuppies.

Birds seem to be on every tree branch and fence post in Indiana. The cardinal is the official state bird. A few of the other common birds include robins, orioles, starlings, swallows, bluebirds, and sparrows.

Indiana's rivers, streams, and lakes shelter fish of many kinds. They include bass, catfish, trout, gar, sunfish, darter, pike, perch, and crappie.

There are many coyotes in Indiana.

Box Turtle

Raccoon

Mudpuppy

History

Indiana was first controlled by tribes belonging mainly to the Miami Nation of Native Americans. Later, France was the first European country to explore and settle the area.

French adventurers built forts in the early 1700s near the present-day cities of Fort Wayne, Lafayette, and Vincennes.

Fort Wayne was named after General Anthony Wayne of the U.S. Army.

After a long war, Great Britain took control of Indiana from the French in 1763. Britain went to war again in 1775 against its rebellious colonies in America. This time it was Great Britain that lost. Indiana became part of the newly formed United States.

George Rogers Clark was a Revolutionary War leader who moved his troops across the cold Wabash River to surprise and capture a British fort at Vincennes, Indiana, in 1779.

During the late 1780s, Indiana was part of a large region called the Northwest Territory. Many Native Americans did not like sharing their land with new settlers. Fighting began, and the United States Army was called in to chase away the Indians. Instead, the soldiers were defeated. More soldiers were sent to try again. Led by General "Mad" Anthony Wayne, they finally won in 1794.

The Northwest Territory was divided into several smaller territories in the early 1800s. One of those was called Indiana Territory. Indiana became a state on December 11, 1816. It was the 19th state to enter the Union.

An 1881 map of Indiana.

In the fall of 1811, General William Harrison led about 1,000 U.S. Army and militia troops. They gathered near the Native American village of Prophetstown, near the Tippecanoe River, in Indiana Territory. The Indians' leader, Shawnee Chief Tecumseh, was out of the area. Tecumseh's brother, Tenskwatawa, known as the Prophet, went against his brother's wishes and ordered an early morning attack on November 7, 1811. The U.S. Army suffered the death or wounding of 190 men. The Indians also suffered great losses, and were forced to flee. This became known as the Battle of Tippecanoe.

In the mid-1800s, Indiana became an important center of trade and transportation. The state has a good location along the Ohio River, with access to Lake Michigan. Indiana's vast farmlands also made it a key source of food for the rapidly spreading nation.

The Civil War divided the country in 1861. Indiana fought on the side of the Union North because it was a state against slavery.

Indiana began to industrialize after the Civil War. The invention of the automobile in the 1890s brought many carmakers to Indiana. The state's first steel mill opened in 1906. It helped feed the automobile factories' hunger for metal.

Elwood Haynes of Kokomo, Indiana, with the help of machine shop owners Elmer and Edgar Apperson, built the Haynes "Pioneer" automobile in 1894.

America entered World War I in 1917. Indiana helped win that war by churning out the many items soldiers and sailors needed for battle. The state did the same thing on an even larger scale when the United States was swept into World War II in 1941.

Indiana enjoyed much prosperity after World War II. The good times continued until about 1970, when the economy began to shrink. But Indiana is a state that knows how to turn difficulties into fresh beginnings. It wasn't long before Indiana was once again growing.

Supporting the war effort, a woman works as a welder in an Indiana steel mill in 1942.

Did You Know?

- The world gets 90 percent of its popcorn from Indiana.

- Disneyland was not America's first theme park. The first was Santa Claus Land in Santa Claus, Indiana. It opened in 1946. That was nine years ahead of Disneyland. Santa Claus Land is still around. Today it is called Holiday World.

- Goldfish sold in pet stores are raised on farms. America's first successful fish farm opened in 1899 in Martinsville, Indiana.

Schuyler Colfax

Thomas Hendricks

Charles Fairbanks

Thomas Marshall

Dan Quayle

- Displayed in front of the Putnam County courts building in Greencastle, Indiana, is a captured World War II buzz bomb. Buzz bombs were invented by Nazi Germany. They were the first guided missiles. They were called buzz bombs because of the terrifying buzzing sound made by their jet engines.

- Five United States vice presidents were former governors, U.S. senators, or members of the House of Representatives from Indiana. They included Schuyler Colfax (served 1869-1873); Thomas A. Hendricks (1885); Charles W. Fairbanks (1905-1909); Thomas R. Marshall (1913-1921); and Dan Quayle (1989-1993).

DID YOU KNOW?

People

James Dean (1931-1955) was one of America's most important film actors. He brought modern "teenage cool" to the big screen. Many young movie stars today still copy his acting style. Dean's career was very short. He made only three movies before being killed in a car crash. Dean was born in Marion, Indiana.

Benjamin Harrison

(1833-1901) was the 23rd president of the United States. He served from 1889-1893. Before that, he was a U.S. senator from Indiana. During the Civil War, he was a brigadier general in the Union army. Harrison's grandfather was William Henry Harrison, the ninth president of the United States. Benjamin Harrison was born in North Bend, Ohio, but moved to Indiana when he was 21 years old and called it home until his death.

Orville Redenbacher

(1907-1995) wanted to invent the perfect popcorn. He grew many different types of corn for popping before finding the one that is sold under his name in supermarkets today. Orville Redenbacher's Gourmet Popping Corn first became available in 1969. Redenbacher himself starred in television commercials for the product. In them, he always looked like a cross between a scientist and a nerd because of his horn-rimmed glasses, bow tie, and suspenders. He was born in Brazil, Indiana.

Larry Bird (1956-) is a famous National Basketball Association player. Bird was born in West Baden, Indiana. He grew up in Indiana, and went to Indiana State University. In 1978, he was drafted by the Boston Celtics. He played forward, winning

many NBA awards. Bird led the Celtics to three NBA Championships before retiring in 1992. In 1997, Bird went back to Indiana, accepting the job of head coach of the Indiana Pacers. He was named NBA Coach of the Year in 1998, and led the team to the Eastern Conference Championship in 2000. Today, he is president of basketball operations for the Pacers.

Cities

Indianapolis is the capital of Indiana. It has a population of 795,458. Founded in the early 1820s, the city is located in the center of the state. Indianapolis is known as the Racing Capital of the World. That is because

Indianapolis is the largest city in Indiana.

it is where the Indianapolis 500 automobile race is held every Memorial Day weekend. The Indianapolis 500 is a tradition that dates back to the time when Indianapolis was the nation's most important city for the making of cars. Today, Indianapolis is a city with many types of industries and business.

Fort Wayne is Indiana's second-largest city. Its population is 251,247. Fort Wayne is located near the Ohio border. It is called Fort Wayne in honor of the general who fought Native Americans in the late 1790s. Today, Fort Wayne is an important center of manufacturing, insurance, communications, transportation, and technology.

Fort Wayne is known as the Summit City because when a canal was built in the 1830s, the city was the highest point along the canal's route.

Evansville is the third-largest city in Indiana. Its population is 116,253. It's called the River City because it is located along the Ohio River in the southwest corner of the state. Evansville is named in honor of a hero of the War of 1812. The economy of Evansville today is built on financial services, health care, retailing, entertainment, and transportation.

Evansville is called the River City because it's next to the Ohio River.

Notre Dame's Golden Dome. Many people come to South Bend to see it.

South Bend is Indiana's fourth-largest city. It has a population of 104,069. South Bend is located near the border with Michigan in north-central Indiana. Education is important in South Bend. The city is the home of the famous University of Notre Dame. Also important to the city's economy are electronics manufacturing, technology, and health care.

Steel making is an important activity in **Gary**, Indiana. It is the state's fifth-largest city. Gary's population is 96,429. The city is considered a suburb of neighboring Chicago, Illinois, which is just 25 miles (40 km) away.

A steel-making plant in Gary.

Transportation

Many products are shipped in and out of Indiana from a deep-water port on Lake Michigan, and from two major ports along the Ohio River. The Lake Michigan port is called Burns Harbor. It is

Iron ore is unloaded into waiting train cars at a dock on Lake Michigan at Burns Harbor, Indiana.

near the town of Portage. The two Ohio River ports are the Southwind Maritime Center in Mount Vernon, and the Clark Maritime Center in Jeffersonville. About 70 million tons (64 million metric tons) of cargo are put aboard ships and barges each year.

Indiana has more than 90,000 miles (144,841 km) of roads, streets, and highways.

Railroads have been important to Indiana since the late 1840s. There are more than 4,200 miles (6,759 km) of tracks connecting Indiana's ports with cities across the state. The tracks are mostly used by freight trains. More than half of what they haul is coal.

The state's major airports are Indianapolis International, Evansville Regional, Fort Wayne International, South Bend Regional, and Gary-Chicago International.

A jet flies past the control tower at Indianapolis International Airport. More than 8.5 million passengers travel from the airport each year.

Natural Resources

Almost two-thirds of Indiana is farmland. The most important crop grown on the state's 59,000 farms is corn. The next most important crop is soybeans. Many hogs are raised on Indiana farms.

Corn is harvested on an Indiana farm.

Forests cover about one-fifth of Indiana. More than 90 percent of those forests are used as a source of wood for houses, furniture, and other products. Most of these timberlands are in the southern half of the state.

The outside of New York's famous Empire State Building is covered in 200,000 cubic feet (5,663 cubic meters) of Indiana limestone.

Limestone is used to dress up the outside of expensive homes and office buildings. Many agree that the best limestone in America comes from southern Indiana. Other treasures from the mines and quarries of Indiana are masonry cement, gypsum, and coal.

Industry

Many things are made in Indiana. These include musical instruments, motors, batteries, tires, cars, medicine, electronics, and steel. More steel is made in northwestern Indiana than anywhere else in the nation.

Sparks fly as a steel train rail is manufactured in an Indiana steel mill.

Indiana is part of a northeastern United States region called the Manufacturing Belt. Hard times fell on this region in the 1970s and 1980s.

Many United States factories could no longer compete against less-expensive companies in other parts of the world. Many were forced out of business. In Indiana, most factories have remained open and busy. The reason is that Indiana tries to help its companies be competitive with the rest of the world.

Indiana's friendliness to business is attracting many new types of companies. These include technology companies, information services, and large financial firms.

The Nestle Bunny points to the company's Anderson, Indiana, facility. Nestles plans to expand its business in this location.

Sports

An Indy 500 race in the early 1900s.

The famous Indianapolis 500 race is run every May. It is a 500-mile (805-km) race, which equals 200 times around the track.

The Indianapolis 500 automobile race takes place every May in Indiana. As many as 400,000 people jam into the Indianapolis Motor Speedway to watch the race, which lasts 200 laps. It is called the "500" because 200 times around the track equals 500 miles (805 km). But the contest does not actually take place in Indianapolis. It's held in a town called Speedway, which is surrounded by Indianapolis. The first Indy 500 was held in 1911.

Pacers

Indiana has two major professional sports teams. They are football's Indianapolis Colts and basketball's Indiana Pacers. Both teams have huge numbers of fans.

Also loved in Indiana is high school and college basketball. The two colleges that usually receive the most attention from fans are Indiana University and the University of Notre Dame.

Indiana University fans are the Hoosiers.

Notre Dame fans are called the Fighting Irish.

Entertainment

Many important American painters and sculptors have come from Indiana. The state has more than 400 organizations for the celebration of art in all its many forms. Indiana is home to a number of ballet troupes, opera companies, stage theaters, and film festivals.

Museums are found in every major city of Indiana. A

fun place is The Children's Museum of Indianapolis. It has the Fireworks of Glass, a 43-foot (13-m) -tall blown glass sculpture, the SpaceQuest Planetarium, and many dinosaur fossils.

A robotic *T-Rex* stands at the Children's Museum of Indianapolis.

Indiana has more than 20 symphony orchestras. Every summer there is an event called the Midwest Music Summit. It takes place in Indianapolis. The city also hosts a major jazz festival.

Blues guitarist B.B. King plays during a music performance at the Indy Jazz Fest.

Timeline

5000 BC—First humans arrive in Indiana. They later unite as members of the Miami Nation.

1700s—France begins exploring and building forts in Indiana.

1783—The United States gains control of Indiana. More settlers come to the state.

1790s—Settlers and Native Americans fight.

1816—Indiana becomes the 19th state.

1840s—Indiana becomes important as a trade and transportation state.

1861-65—The American Civil War is fought. Indiana stays with the Union, fighting on the side of the North.

1890s—Automobile invented. Carmakers flock to Indiana to set up factories.

1906—First Indiana steel mill opens.

1950s—Indiana enters a time of great economic success.

1970s—Hard times hit the state.

1990s—Indiana bounces back with new ways of becoming successful.

2007—The Indianapolis Colts win Super Bowl XLI.

Glossary

Blizzard—A severe snowstorm made worse by high winds.

Civil War—The American war fought between the Northern and Southern states from 1861-1865. The Southern states were for slavery. They wanted to start their own country. Northern states fought against slavery and a division of the country.

Glacier—A large mass of ice built up by snow that falls and does not melt at the end of winter. Glaciers can grow taller than a mountain and extend for hundreds or thousands of miles during an ice age.

Gypsum—A white or light grey mineral that is used to make cements and plasters, such as plaster of Paris.

Industrialize—To change a society or location from one in which work is done mainly by hand to one in which work is done mainly by machines.

Planetarium—A theater that projects the nighttime sky on a rounded ceiling, allowing people to view stars, comets, and other objects in space.

World War I—A war that was fought in Europe from 1914 to 1918, involving countries around the world. The United States entered the war in April 1917.

World War II—A conflict across the world, lasting from 1939-1945. The United States entered the war after the Japanese military bombed the American naval base at Pearl Harbor, Hawaii, in December 1941.

Index

A
America (*See* United States)
Army, U.S. 20

B
Bird, Larry 29
Boston Celtics 29
Brazil, IN 28
Burns Harbor 34

C
Chicago, IL 33
Children's Museum of Indianapolis, The 42
Civil War 22, 27
Clark Maritime Center 34
Colfax, Schuyler 25
Collegeville, IN 13

D
Dean, James 26
Disneyland 24

E
Eastern Conference Championship 29
Eel River 11
Evansville, IN 32
Evansville Regional Airport 35

F
Fairbanks, Charles 25
Fireworks of Glass 42
Fort Wayne, IN 18, 31
Fort Wayne International Airport 35
France 18

G
Gary, IN 33
Gary-Chicago International Airport 35
Germany 25
Great Britain 18
Great Lakes 11
Greencastle, IN 25

H
Harrison, Benjamin 27
Harrison, William Henry 27
Hendricks, Thomas 25
Holiday World 24

I
Illinois 33
Indiana Pacers 29, 41
Indiana State University 29
Indiana Territory 20
Indiana University 41
Indianapolis, IN 30, 40, 43
Indianapolis 500 30, 40
Indianapolis Colts 41
Indianapolis International Airport 35
Indianapolis Motor Speedway 40

J
Jeffersonville, IN 34

K
Kankakee River 11
Kentucky 10

L
Lafayette, IN 18

M
Manufacturing Belt 38
Marion, IN 26
Marshall, Thomas 25
Martinsville, IN 24
Maumee River 11
Miami (tribe) 18
Michigan 33
Michigan, Lake 11, 22, 34
Midwest 8
Midwest Music Summit 43
Mississinewa River 11
Mount Vernon, IN 34

N
National Basketball Association (NBA) 29
NBA Championship 29
NBA Coach of the Year 29
New Whiteland, IN 13
North Bend, OH 27
Northwest Territory 20

O
Ohio 27, 31
Ohio River 10, 22, 32, 34
Orville Redenbacher's Gourmet Popping Corn 28

P
Portage, IN 34
Putnam County 25

Q
Quayle, Dan 25

R
Redenbacher, Orville 28

S
Santa Claus, IN 24
Santa Claus Land 24
South Bend, IN 33
South Bend Regional Airport 35
Southwind Maritime Center 34
SpaceQuest Planetarium 42
Speedway, IN 40

T
Tippecanoe River 11

U
Union 20, 22
Union army 27
United States 8, 18, 20, 23, 24, 25, 26, 27, 37, 38, 39
University of Notre Dame 33, 41

V
Vincennes, IN 18

W
Wabash River 8
Wawasee, Lake 11
Wayne, Anthony 20
West Baden, IN 29
White River 11
Whitewater River 11
World War I 23
World War II 23, 25